Adult Child of Hippies

Adult Child of Hippies

Willow Yamauchi

INSOMNIAC PRESS

Library and Archives Canada Cataloguing in Publication

Yamauchi, Willow
Adult child of hippies / Willow Yamauchi.

ISBN 978-1-897415-24-5

1. Hippies--Canada. 2. Hippies--Canada--Humor.
3. Hippies--Canada--Pictorial works. I. Title.

HM647.Y24 2010   305.5'68   C2010-904608-0

The publisher gratefully acknowledges the support of the
Canada Council, the Ontario Arts Council and the Depart-
ment of Canadian Heritage through the Book Publishing
Industry Development Program.

Printed and bound in Canada

Insomniac Press
520 Princess Avenue,
London, Ontario, Canada, N6B 2B8
www.insomniacpress.com

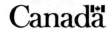

Special thanks to all of the present and former Hippies and Adult Children of Hippies who shared their pictures and stories.

Enduring thanks and love to
my own family—
Ron, Sophie and Flynn;
to the cover girl—my sister Rachel;
and to our mother, Sharon.

Introduction

Do you have a name such as Willow, River, Oak, or Sunshine? Have you ever lived on a commune, or done yoga naked with your family? If yes, then you are an Adult Child of Hippies (ACOH). Adult Children of Hippies grew up in extreme conditions: eating sprouts, and lugging herbal tea in their Thermoses to school (if they were fortunate enough to make it to school). ACOHs were born and brought up mostly in the Seventies and Eighties. As their parents revelled in the counterculture, ACOHs struggled with basic hygiene, not to mention broader social acceptance. Until now, this group has not been represented in the media. Content with leaving the past in the past, ACOHs have successfully blended into the mainstream; but the memories and photos persist. Finally, Willow Yamauchi has brought her generational subculture into the light. We no longer need to feel alone or ashamed or our bizarre heritage. Take the test, see the pictures, and stand up tall!

Say it: I am an Adult Child of Hippies... and I am proud.

1.
You felt that going back to the land was a
noble and realistic goal.

❏

2.
You were ever "home-schooled"
or "un-schooled".

❏

3.
A Volkswagen bus makes you nostalgic for
your childhood home.

❏

Bonus Mark
*You replaced the VW with a peace sign,
painted it like a rainbow, and gave it a
groovy name.*

❏

4.
You knew people who lived in teepees.

❑

Bonus Mark
They were your family.

❑

5.
You knew people who ate
their own placenta.

❏

Bonus Mark
*They were vegans who referred to it as
"unkilled meat."*

❏

6.

You have to tell your children not to
mention the special plants growing in
Grandma's garden.

❑

7.
You know people who make
soap and candles for a living.

❑

8.
Your favourite fragrances were patchouli,
sandalwood, and musk.

❏

Bonus Mark
*And you used them for
massage, outdoors*

❏

Double Bonus Marks
In the nude.

❏

9.
You shared your house with livestock.

❏

10.
You lived on a commune.

❏

Bonus Mark
*It had a name containing the words creative,
contemplative, or intentional.*

❏

11.
You shared a community garden with other hippie families.

❏

Bonus Mark
You had your own patch.

❏

12.
When you grew up you wanted to be
a draft dodger.

13.
You have a parent whose recipe for
marijuana beer is legendary.

❏

14.
You slaughtered your own pigs.

❏

Bonus Mark
You used the tail to grease your frying pan.

❏

15.
You have eaten bear.

❏

16.
You lived on a boat or float house.

❏

Bonus Mark
And it was up on stilts.

❏

Double Bonus Marks
And it sank.

❏

17.
You felt tie-dye and batik were valid fashion
choices.

❏

18.
You had the most normal name of all your
friends, and it was Willow.

❑

19.
You wore a bag of small stones around your
neck that you drew power from, likely
containing a minimum of amber, cat's eye,
and turquoise.

❏

Bonus Mark
*It was either made from leather or was
rainbow coloured.*

❏

20.
You were breastfed by
at least two different people.

❏

Bonus Mark
And they weren't related to you.

❏

21.
You were thrown into a near panic as
Father's Day approached due to an unclear
grasp of your own paternity.

❏

22.
Your family celebrated important events
with a communal fire-walk.

❏

23.
You say, "Oh my Goddess" reflexively, not wanting to offend the Earth Goddess with patriarchal utterances.

❏

24.
You celebrated the winter solstice and vernal equinox instead of Christmas and Easter.

❏

Bonus Mark
And your parents lectured you on how Christianity co-opted these celebrations.

❏

25.
You believed that the only hairstyles were
long and tousled or long and braided.

❏

26.
If and when you went to San Francisco,
you would, without doubt,
wear flowers in your hair.

❑

27.
You regularly visited a nudist colony.

❑

28.
You believed clothing was
a sign of repression.

29.
You actually liked carob.

❑

30.
Your dad's hair was longer than your
mom's.

❏

Bonus Mark
He also had a long beard.

❏

Double Bonus Marks
And he tied it in a knot.

❏

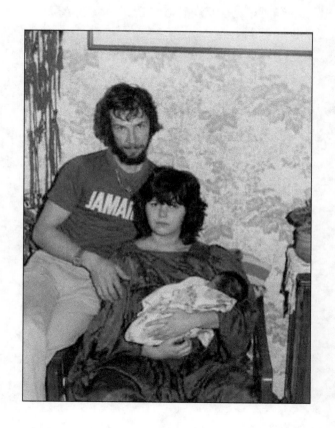

31.
You attended a Gestalt group
with your family.

❏

Bonus Mark
*People felt it was beautiful how you
expressed yourself.*

❏

32.
You instinctively knew the difference
between "Northern Lights,"
"Maui Wowie," and "Red Hair."

❏

33.
Your butter knives were scorched black,
and everyone knew why.

❏

34.
The phrase, "off the grid"
brings back panicky feelings.

❏

35.
You saw stinging nettles as a
delicious side dish.

❏

36.

You can't find your childhood friends on Facebook, because they all changed their names to something normal.

❏

37.
You had a genuine fear of being eaten by
cougars and bears.

❏

38.
You were a vegetarian
but really "dug" Wavy Gravy.

❑

39.
You cross referenced your Chinese birth
year with your astrological sign
reflexively to come up with your own
unique personality template.

❏

40.
You believed that "the Man" was
trying to control you via your Social
Insurance Number and therefore bartered
goods to avoid detection.

❏

41.
Your family tossed the I Ching
during "family meetings" for guidance.

44.
You use the phrase, "down to stems and
seeds" to mean "times are tough."

❑

45.
You chewed licorice roots as a treat.

❑

46.

You chanted, "Hey, hey LBJ, how many kids did you kill today?" instead of schoolyard rhymes.

❏

47.
You toasted marshmallows
on a kerosene lamp.

❏

Bonus Mark
For breakfast!

❏

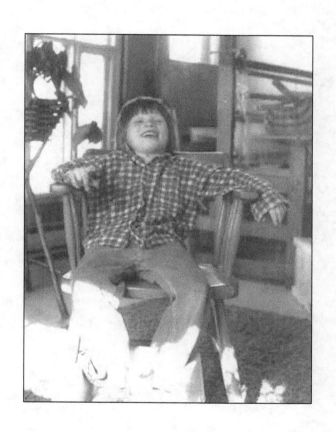

48.
You were jealous of people
who had electricity.

❏

49.
You knew which incense sticks best mask
marijuana smoke at an early age.

❏

50.
You breast-fed until grade school.

❑

51.
You felt beaded curtains were a reasonable
alternative to doors.

❏

52.
You had a menstruation party upon
menarche.

❏

53.
You were overly emotionally
involved in Bob Dylan and Joan Baez's
love affair and subsequent break-up.

❏

54.
You took your first hit of acid with a parent.

❏

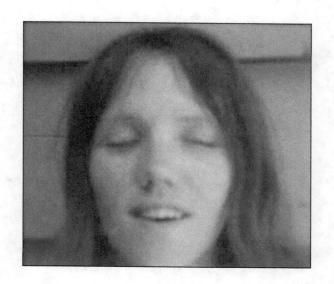

55.
You have bathed in public
washrooms while your family "camped" in
the parking lot of the mall.

❏

56.
You practiced yoga daily as a family.

❏

Bonus Mark
In the nude!

❏

57.
You thought macramé was groovy.

❏

Bonus Mark
Because you made it.

❏

58.
You knew how to find psilocybin
mushrooms (sillies) in a field and could
reflexively tell them apart from other,
similar looking, though entirely deadly
mushrooms that often grew
adjacent to them.

❏

59.
You were taught to loathe and fear
McDonald's,
but secretly ate there as an act of rebellion.

❏

60.
You regularly did cleansing fasts.

❏

Bonus Mark
They included thimbleberry leaves, cayenne,
and/or honey.

❏

61.
When you grew up you wanted to be
Carlos Castaneda.

❏

62.
You wore a "mac" jacket and "gumboots"
to school.

❏

63.
You hung your toilet seat by the wood stove
so it would be toasty on winter nights when
you took it out to the outhouse.

❑

64.
You could "sex" pot plants by the time
you were five.

❑

65.
You knew from an early age that any
psychedelic trip needed a "trip master,"
and you could list
a minimum of three trip masters.

❏

66.
You have been in more saunas
than grocery stores.

❏

67.
You were extremely conscious and
somewhat anxious about the dawning of the
"Age of Aquarius."

❏

68.

You thought underwear was repressive and stopped your genitals from being able to "breathe."

❏

69.
Your ability to split kindling in
the dark earned you heavy praise
from your family.

❏

70.
You referred to shoplifting as
"liberating."

❏

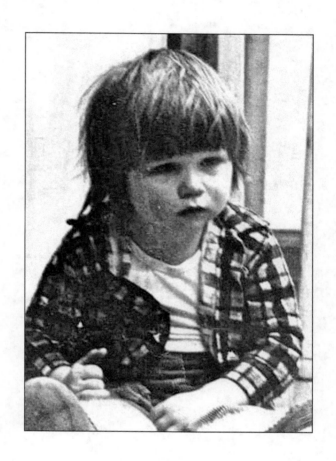

71.
You made comfrey poultices
to treat insect bites.

❏

72.
Your parents have more tattoos than you do.

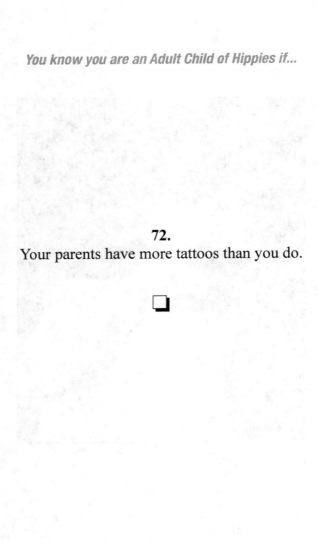

73.
You attended rallies in front of churches
but never actually set foot
into one.

◻

74.
You referred to your period as your
"moon time."

❏

75.
Your parents slept with all your friends'
parents and everyone was "cool" with it.

❑

76.
You teethed on your
mother's love beads.

❑

77.
Your colouring books were
Tibetan mandalas.

❏

Bonus Mark
*You recycled crayons by melting them into
crayon rainbows.*

❏

78.
You considered granola to be junk food due
to the large amount of honey in it.

❏

79.
You never knew that people were
allowed to pay to get into folk festivals.

❏

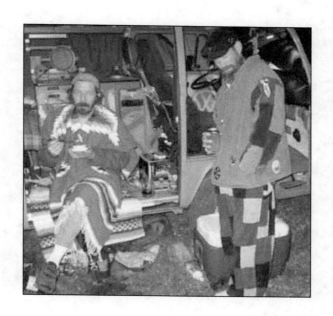

80.
You felt that Haight-Ashbury
was a "sell out."

❏

81.
You went barefoot year round unless there
was snow, when you would reluctantly don
moccasins or gumboots.

❏

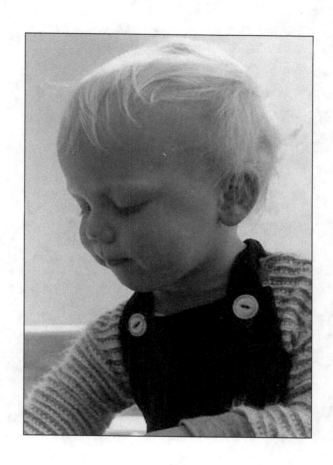

82.
You knew the difference between a
"happening" and an "experience"
a "love in" and, of course, a "be in."

❏

83.
You went to friends' houses to have a bath
or shower.

❑

Bonus Mark
You did it as a family to "save water."

❑

84.
You earnestly believed Peter, Paul, and
Mary were a threesome, not a trio.

❏

85.
You instinctively knew how to "combine
grains" to make a "complete protein."

❏

86.
You wished you had your own guru in India.

❏

Bonus Mark
You had friends with their own guru in India.

❏

Double Bonus Marks
And they changed their name to whatever the guru named them and wore only the colours red and orange.

❏

87.
You saw Cat Stevens as a mistreated hero.

❏

88.
You planned to take mescaline as soon as
possible to find your "animal guide."

❑

Bonus Mark
You thought it was either a puma or a wolf.

❑

89.
You considered the eating of honey to be
abusive to bees.

❏

90.
You collected pretty LSD blotters
instead of stickers.

91.
You referred to getting arrested as getting
"popped" or "busted."

❑

Bonus Mark
*The first time you were "popped" or
"busted" was with a parent.*

❑

92.
You attended sweat lodges with
your parents.

❏

Bonus Mark
You had your own sweat lodge.

❏

Double Bonus Marks
Because your parents were "shamans."

❏

93.
Your entire understanding of
Christianity came from watching
Jesus Christ, Superstar.

❏

94.
You refer to any gathering as an
"experience."

❏

95.
You chanted the words to
"Hare Krishna" with the other
neighbourhood children.

❏

98.
You had a long-term plan to camp in
Goa for a year.

❏

99.
You were jealous of your friends who had their own tai chi master living with them.

❑

100.
You owned and used tarot cards.

❏

101.
You participated in group therapy.

❏

Bonus Mark
*It included primal scream
and/or rebirthing.*

❏

102.
You were taught that dancing to music
involves a complete body twirling,
swaying, and orgiastic flailing.

❏

Bonus Mark
*You practiced the art of
the whirling Dervish and Sufi.*

❏

103.
You felt Stonehenge was your
spiritual base.

❑

104.
You felt refrigeration was highly overrated.

❏

105.
You knew the difference between "dropping out" and "dropping sid."

❏

106.
You shaved your legs as an act of rebellion.

❏

107.
You closely aligned yourself
with your astrological sign and
made common reference to your
"sun sign" and "rising sign."

❏

110.
You knew the difference between
grass and *grass*.

❏

113.
You could clearly differentiate
between an "open relationship," an
"understanding," and "swinging."

❏

Bonus Mark
Because your family practiced them.

❏

116.
Your family practiced "healing touch"
when you were ill.

❏

Bonus Mark
It involved "channelling white light."

❏

117.
You ended grace with the phrases,
"merry meet" and/or "blessed be."

118.
You referred to the Earth (goddess) as Gaia.

❏

119.
You bathed in small basins
to conserve water.

❏

122.
You refer to your female private parts
as your "yoni."

❏

125.
You've never actually seen
your father's face due to
heavy beard infestation.

126.
Your family switched to "Bragg's" from "soya sauce" as soya didn't have the same "amino acids."

❏

127.

You treated infestations of pin-worms with garlic, and infestations of lice with kerosene.

❑

128.
Your family has a heavy reliance on squash
and rutabagas.

❑

129.
You were extremely concerned
state of your "karma

Bonus M

You would do a "k
to regain karm
after mak

You know you are an Adult Child of Hippies if...

130.
You hoped someday to have your own yurt,
or, better yet, house truck!

☐

131.
You were extremely concerned about reincarnation and believed that your deceased animals and relatives were "reborn" after "passing over to the other side."

❑

132.
You knew that any gathering
involved at least one teepee, one VW van,
and a great big pot of tabouli.

❏

133.
You knew that if you ever had to
communicate via rifle due to lack of
telephone, remember, three shots means
SOS!

❏

134.
You always
stopped to smell the roses.

❏

135.
Your parents felt that power tools were an
appropriate plaything.

❏

136.
You thought all loaves of bread
weighed over five pounds.

❑

50 and less

You likely have dreadlocks and participate in drum circles. You have recently purchased a Splitty VW bus and are planning on being an activist and professional "gardener." You only shop in thrift stores and are considering becoming vegan or—better yet—fruitarian. You dream of creating an agrarian-based utopia on an island. Your parents wonder where they went wrong, and your children, Goddess help them, will also need the ongoing support of ACOH in the future.